CI   ER

PRESENTED TO PARLIAMENT BY
THE PRIME MINISTER
BY COMMAND OF HER MAJESTY,
JULY 1991

LONDON: HMSO
£8.50 net

Cm 1599

354.410099
CIT

FOREWORD

1054576 ✗

I take great pleasure in the first set of initiatives under the Citizen's Charter. To make public services answer better to the wishes of their users, and to raise their quality overall, have been ambitions of mine ever since I was a local councillor in Lambeth over 20 years ago.

In the 1980s, reforms in schools, housing and hospitals gave people more say in how their services are run. Privatisation and contracting-out have transformed performance. The programme we are publishing today carries these reforms further - and into new territory. I want the Citizen's Charter to be one of the central themes of public life in the 1990s.

For this White Paper is only a beginning. Over the coming months, Ministers will be bringing forward more detailed plans for each service. But today we provide some early examples of how the principles of the Charter will be applied. How we will, for example, be introducing guaranteed maximum waiting times for hospital operations. How we will require all schools to provide parents with reports. How British Rail will be introducing new compensation schemes for poor service. How those who regulate electricity, water, gas and telecommunications will be given the same strong powers to insist on good service standards for the customer. How we will toughen up inspection and audit, relate pay more closely to performance, and provide the citizen with more and better information.

The Citizen's Charter is about giving more power to the citizen. But citizenship is about our responsibilities - as parents, for example, or as neighbours - as well as our entitlements. The Citizen's Charter is not a recipe for more state action; it is a testament of our belief in people's right to be informed and choose for themselves.

The White Paper sets out the mechanics for improving choice, quality, value and accountability. Not all apply to every service. But all have a common objective: to raise the standard of public services, up to and beyond the best at present available.

There is a well-spring of talent, energy, care and commitment in our public services. The aim of the Citizen's Charter is to release these qualities. Then we will have services in which the citizen can have confidence, and all public servants can have pride.

John Major

20/8/92 (9)

CONTENTS

INTRODUCTION

All public services are paid for by individual citizens, either directly or through their taxes. They are entitled to expect high-quality services, responsive to their needs, provided efficiently at a reasonable cost. Where the state is engaged in regulating, taxing or administering justice, these functions too must be carried out fairly, effectively and courteously.

This Government continues to uphold the central principle that essential services – such as education and health – must be available to all, irrespective of means. And its consistent aim has been to increase choice, extend competition and thereby improve quality in all services.

In a free market, competing firms must strive to satisfy their customers, or they will not prosper. Where choice and competition are limited, consumers cannot as easily or effectively make their views count. In many public services, therefore, we need to increase both choice and competition where we can; but we also need to develop other ways of ensuring good standards of service.

Many of Britain's key industries and public services have been privatised in the last decade. This has been done in a way which promotes direct competition between providers as far as possible. Where elements of monopoly remain, regulation protects the consumer.

Choice can also be extended within the public sector. When the public sector remains responsible for a function it can introduce competition and pressure for efficiency by contracting with the private sector for its provision.

Finally, choice can be restored by introducing alternative forms of provision, and creating a wider range of options wherever that is cost-effective. This has been a key objective, for example, of reforms in housing and education.

Through the Citizen's Charter the Government is now determined to drive reforms further into the core of the public services, extending the benefits of choice, competition, and commitment to service more widely.

The Citizen's Charter is the most comprehensive programme ever to raise quality, increase choice, secure better value, and extend accountability. We believe that it will set a pattern, not only for Britain, but for other countries of the world.

The Charter programme will be pursued in a number of ways. The approach will vary from service to service in different parts of the United Kingdom. The Citizen's Charter is not a blueprint which imposes a drab and uniform pattern on every service. It is a toolkit of initiatives and ideas to raise standards in the way most appropriate to each service.

The Charter programme will be at the heart of government policy in the 1990s. Quality of service to the public, and the new pride that it will give to the public servants who provide it, will be a central theme.

There are four main themes in the White Paper:

QUALITY – A sustained new programme for improving the quality of public services.

CHOICE – Choice, wherever possible between competing providers, is the best spur to quality improvement.

STANDARDS – The citizen must be told what service standards are and be able to act where service is unacceptable.

VALUE – The citizen is also a taxpayer; public services must give value for money within a tax bill the nation can afford.

The range of mechanisms in the Charter covers:

- more privatisation;

- wider competition;

- further contracting-out;

- more performance-related pay;

- published performance targets – local and national;

- comprehensive publication of information on standards achieved;

- more effective complaints procedures;

- tougher and more independent inspectorates;

- better redress for the citizen when services go badly wrong.

THE PRINCIPLES OF PUBLIC SERVICE

Every citizen is entitled to expect:

- **Standards**
  Explicit standards, published and prominently displayed at the point of delivery. These standards should invariably include courtesy and helpfulness from staff, accuracy in accordance with statutory entitlements, and a commitment to prompt action, which might be expressed in terms of a target response or waiting time. If targets are to be stretched, it may not be possible to guarantee them in every case; minimum, as well as average, standards may be necessary. There should be a clear presumption that standards will be progressively improved as services become more efficient.

- **Openness**
  There should be no secrecy about how public services are run, how much they cost, who is in charge, and whether or not they are meeting their standards. Public servants should not be anonymous. Save only where there is a real threat to their safety, all those who deal directly with the public should wear name badges and give their name on the telephone and in letters.

- **Information**
  Full, accurate information should be readily available, in plain language, about what services are being provided. Targets should be published, together with full and audited information about the results achieved. Wherever possible, information should be in comparable form, so that there is a pressure to emulate the best.

- **Choice**
  The public sector should provide choice wherever practicable. The people affected by services should be consulted. Their views about the services they use should be sought regularly and systematically to inform decisions about what services should be provided.

- **Non-discrimination**
  Services should be available regardless of race or sex. Leaflets are being printed in minority languages where there is a need. In Wales public bodies are aware of the needs of Welsh speakers.

- **Accessibility**
  Services should be run to suit the convenience of customers, not staff. This means flexible opening hours, and telephone inquiry points that direct callers quickly to someone who can help them.

- **And if things go wrong?**
  At the very least, the citizen is entitled to a good explanation, or an apology. He or she should be told **why** the train is late, or **why** the doctor could not keep the appointment. There should be a well-publicised and readily available complaints procedure. If there is a serious problem, it should be put right. And lessons must be learnt so that mistakes are not repeated. Nobody wants to see money diverted from service improvement into large-scale compensation for indifferent services. But the Government intends to introduce new forms of redress where these can be made to stimulate rather than distract from efficiency.

Scope

The Citizen's Charter applies to all public services. These include government departments and agencies, nationalised industries, local authorities, the NHS, the courts, police and emergency services. In the private sector, it covers the key utilities; it does not encompass wider consumer protection law.

Cost

The Government remains committed to a sound public expenditure and tax policy. Total public spending has fallen as a share of national income. Within this framework extra taxpayers' money has been put into key services. For example, in the past ten years the level of spending on education has increased by nearly 13 per cent in real terms and that on health and personal social services by 27 per cent. The cost of these services for each adult member of the population is now around £620 a year for education and £740 for health and personal social services. In all, public spending amounts to some £5,000 per adult each year. We shall continue to put more resources into priority public services whenever extra money can be afforded. The Charter programme is about finding better ways of converting the money that can be afforded into even better services.

Charter Standard and Chartermark

We will publish a new standard for the delivery of quality in public services – the Charter Standard. The key principles will be:

- Publication of the standards of service that the customer can reasonably expect, and of performance against those standards.

- Evidence that the views of those who use the service have been taken into account in setting standards.

- Clear information about the range of services provided, in plain language.

- Courteous and efficient customer service, from staff who are normally prepared to identify themselves by name.

- Well-signposted avenues for complaint if the customer is not satisfied, with some means of independent review wherever possible.

- Independent validation of performance against standards and a clear commitment to improving value for money.

Only those who meet the Charter Standard will be entitled to use the Chartermark.

Implementation

The task is an ambitious one. We are determined to make it happen as quickly as possible. Implementation must be local and specific. It is in the hospital, the school, the police station, and the tax office that the citizen will expect the commitment to raising standards to become a reality.

Services work best where those responsible for providing them can respond directly to the needs of their clients. This White Paper sets the framework and gives some examples of what the new policy will mean in some key areas. It will be followed up by a programme of action across all public services and by detailed charters for patients, parents, passengers, taxpayers, and other groups.

We are determined to ensure that the goals set out in the White Paper are achieved. In some areas reforms are already in place which will form the springboard for implementing the Charter proposals. In other parts of the public sector, employees are dedicated and eager to provide a good service, but are held back by the systems in which they work.

The Government will act swiftly, and will bring forward legislation to remove obstacles, open the way for improvements and strengthen the powers of auditors and regulators. A summary of the proposals in the White Paper is set out after this introduction.

Citizen's Charter Unit and the Prime Minister's panel of advisers

The Prime Minister will appoint a panel of advisers on the Citizen's Charter initiative. A unit will be set up in the Cabinet Office to co-ordinate the programme of action arising from the White Paper.

One of the first tasks will be to convert the Charter principles into generally applicable guidance on the way in which standards should be specified in the public services, taking account of progress already made in the development of codes and practices for quality performance in the field of services.

We will be taking immediate steps to encourage all public services to adopt Charter principles and to apply them to their own operations. Those organisations which feel they have achieved excellence in pursuit of the Citizen's Charter objectives will be able to apply for the Charter Standard and the right to use the Chartermark.

SUMMARY OF PROPOSALS

SETTING STANDARDS OF SERVICE

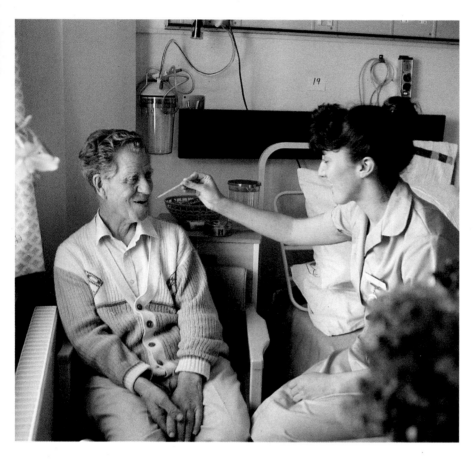

We will build on the NHS reforms later this year by publishing charters in England, Scotland and Wales. These will spell out what the NHS should provide to meet people's needs. **The national charters will set out patients' rights to expect:**

- good quality care;

- clear information about the options available for their care or treatment and continuing information about how each case is developing;

- involvement, as far as is practical, in their own care and treatment;

- choice of GP, including the opportunity to change easily;

- control, with a right to give or withhold consent to medical treatment;

- freedom, with a right to decide whether or not to participate in medical research and student training;

- respect at all times for privacy, dignity, religious and cultural beliefs;

- consideration for relatives and friends visiting or enquiring after patients;

- ability to comment on the care they have received, and to make a formal complaint when they wish;

- access, with safeguards, to information held about them;

- satisfaction if these standards are not achieved.

A CHARTER FOR PATIENTS

The NHS reforms

The aims of the Citizen's Charter lie at the heart of the NHS reforms. They provide for a wider choice for patients, improved responsiveness to their needs and specific standards for patient services. Health authorities must seek local citizens' views on their services.

Telling the public more – the local charters

At local level, and consistent with these national frameworks, health authorities will produce charters specific to their own services. Each health authority's charter will set out the main standards of service it has negotiated in its agreements with hospitals and others. These will be local documents which will inform people about what they can expect. They will be widely available, and displayed prominently in hospitals and other health premises so that people know what they are entitled to, the service targets set, and what has been achieved.

Hospitals will be expected to set out for patients the standards of service they offer. This information should be readily available to all patients before and during their visit to the hospital, and to patients' families who wish to visit them on the wards.

Local circumstances vary. It would not be sensible to set centrally national standards that every health authority would be compelled to adopt.

Local initiative must be supported not stifled. As part of the Citizen's Charter programme, the NHS Management Executive will set out the main areas in which local standards of service must be set, monitored and published on a consistent national basis. Further details, including the list of indicators to be published, will be included in national charters.

The Government's health reforms put people first.

The Citizen's Charter will reinforce this. It will mean:

- *publication of national and local charters providing much more information for the public;*

- *comparative information on the performance of health services;*

- *specific and timed appointments for all out-patients;*

- *maximum waiting time for treatments within the NHS.*

Standards

In future, district health authorities (Health Boards in Scotland) will set standards for service in their contracts with hospitals. They will publish targets for how long their residents will have to wait for admission for treatment.

These targets may well vary between districts and between specialties. But this will be published information and all authorities will want to be able to come up to the standards of the best.

Hospital out-patients' appointments

We will require standards to be set and published for hospital out-patient appointments. The maximum time patients should normally have to wait will be displayed for everyone to see in hospital waiting rooms. Patients who have to wait longer will be told why. In order to deliver this, all hospitals will need proper appointment systems for patients. The practice of calling large numbers of patients for appointments at the same time will end.

Primary health care – ensuring GPs give good service to all patients

Under the health reforms, new GP contracts have been introduced. These make more specific the services that GPs are required to provide:

- a full time GP must be available for at least 26 hours a week at times convenient to patients;

- free health checks must be offered to all new patients;

- similar checks must be offered to anyone who has not attended for three years;

- pensioners over 75 will receive annual health checks if they want them.

Better information and more choice in primary care

The public should be given clear information about the precise services offered by each GP practice in order to help them choose a GP. These include important services for women such as well-women clinics and cervical cancer screening. All GPs must now produce leaflets on their practices and the facilities available. Such leaflets should be available in the surgery and also outside it on request. Changing doctors is now easier, too: the patient simply goes to a new doctor of their choice and asks to be registered. Information will be readily available telling patients how to change doctors.

Dentists' patients are entitled to clear information as well. All patients are now entitled to a treatment plan setting out what is proposed.

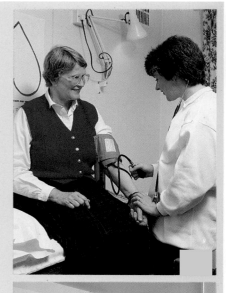

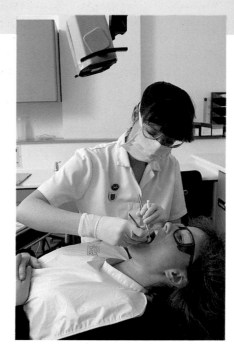

A CHARTER FOR PARENTS

The Government's school reforms have had three key purposes:

- to raise standards in education for all pupils;

- to promote parental influence and choice and widen accountability;

- to achieve better use of resources for pupils.

The Citizen's Charter reinforces these principles and carries them further. It will mean:

- **school reports** on the progress of all pupils, at least annually;

- clear publication of **results achieved** in schools;

- easier **comparison of results** between schools;

- **regular and independent inspection** of all schools with the results reported to parents;

- **more information** to parents to help them to exercise the choice that the education reforms have given them.

We believe that all parents are entitled to expect full information about their children's education in terms of the curriculum, achievements, and management of schools.

Reforms already in place give parents:

- *a **national curriculum** for their children that sets clear objectives backed by national tests showing what each individual child is achieving;*

- *fuller representation on the **governing bodies** of schools;*

- *the right to propose to run their own school, through **grant maintained** status, and a greater say, through **local management**, in how **all** schools are run. More of the management of resources and schools must be transferred from LEAs to within the schools themselves;*

- *more choice, through **open enrolment**, about what schools their children attend, and clearer routes to changing schools;*

- ***more information** to help parents choose a school; more information on how their children are performing, and about how it is possible to change schools.*

These reforms are having a beneficial effect on standards in schools and on parental choice. The Citizen's Charter will guarantee further progress.

More information

i) **We will publish a parents' charter later in the summer.** This will set out clearly parents' rights within schools, the choices they can exercise, and the information about their own school's performance and the performance of other schools which they can obtain from their school, their LEA, and other sources.

ii) **The Audit Commission will be empowered to publish comparative tables** on the efficiency of administration and support services in different local education authorities.

iii) **From 1991/92 all schools, further education and sixth-form colleges will be required to publish their annual public exam results in a common format for each type of institution.** This information will be augmented by the results of tests under the national curriculum as this information becomes available. They will also be required to publish information about placements in further and higher education, as appropriate, and the destination of leavers.

iv) **Schools will also be required, starting with the 1991/92 school year, to publish information on levels of truancy in a common format in their annual reports to parents.** These requirements may later be extended to other items of indicative information about schools' and colleges' performance.

v) **Comparative information on all schools will be required to be collected and published locally.** Parents must also have ready access to information about neighbouring areas so that they are not constrained in making informed choices when selecting schools for their children. The information to be collected and published will include all those items in paras iii) and iv) above.

vi) **From 1991/92 all parents will receive a school report on their child's progress – at least annually. The Government will require all reports to be brought up to a minimum standard within 1991/92.** Subject teachers will assess children's progress in all national curriculum subjects. Head teachers will comment on general development. Reports will also have to say clearly that parents can discuss the contents of the report with a named teacher from the school, and make it clear how and when this discussion can take place. Reports should include results of tests under the national curriculum and enable parents to compare their child's progress with that of others. Reports will provide an opportunity to disseminate other information to parents, for example on curriculum matters, parents' rights and parents' meetings.

Information collected and published has not always reached the parents for whom it is intended. **We will lay a duty on LEAs to disseminate and publish information in accordance with a standard format and will in addition expect LEAs to publish summary comparative results from local schools in local newspapers.** Information on parents' rights and the curriculum should be distributed annually with reports. We will update and reissue the *Guide to the National Curriculum* before the end of this year.

A CHARTER FOR TENANTS

For tenants the Citizen's Charter will mean:

- an improved **Tenants' Charter** for local authority tenants;

- **opportunities for tenants** to transfer away from local authority control;

- a stronger **Tenants' Guarantee** for housing association tenants;

- extending **compulsory competitive tendering** into the field of housing management.

Services for local authority tenants

All housing tenants should benefit from the Citizen's Charter reforms. If your home is provided and maintained by a public sector landlord, it is particularly important that management should be effective and sensitive to your needs. Yet too often local authority housing has seemed remote, impersonal and out of touch with the day-to-day concerns of tenants. Slow and ill-co-ordinated responses to requests for repairs have also been a common source of grievance.

The Right to Buy

The policy of this Government has been to give every tenant who wishes it the right to buy their home. That right has been exercised by more than 1.3 million people in Great Britain since 1979/80. Tough action has been taken against local authorities who resisted or delayed. In the worst cases the Government has powers to take over and see the sale through.

An improved Tenants' Charter

We believe that those who prefer to remain as tenants, or cannot yet afford ownership, should be respected as the valued customers of local authorities. They have to sustain its costs. They have the right to be consulted, to expect high standards and to prompt action when performance is poor.

In 1981 the Government published a national Tenants' Charter. For the first time it set out tenants' rights on such matters as security of tenure, succession of tenancy, exchange, repair and freedom to take lodgers. The charter will now be updated. More streamlined procedures will be introduced so that tenants can enforce their rights under the charter more easily. The new Tenants' Charter will be published later in the year.

Strengthening tenants' rights

With the Citizen's Charter we will be carrying reform of tenants' rights further:

i) **Improving the rights of council tenants to the repair of their homes.**
Council tenants already have a 'right to repair' which allows them to get certain repairs costing up to £200 done where their landlord fails to do so. We are reviewing this right to see how procedures can be simplified and strengthened for the most urgent types of minor repair affecting health, safety or crime prevention.

ii) **Ensuring that all tenants receive information about the standards and performance** of their local authority in housing management. From this year, information will be provided directly to tenants and will cover such key areas as repair times, rent arrears and management costs. This will allow tenants to identify the standards of service they can properly expect, and create pressure for improvement and action where performance is unacceptable.

iii) Encouraging tenants to exercise their right, through a ballot, **to transfer to a new landlord**, such as a housing association.

iv) **Tenants' bids for Housing Action Trusts.**
We already make resources available within the public expenditure plans to allow local authorities, exceptionally, to bid for Housing Action Trusts to take over the ownership and management of the very worst run down estates. In future, where the local authority is reluctant to bid, we will also consider bids for the resources available from tenant groups directly.

v) Encouraging local authorities to introduce **refurbishment contracts,** where contractors and direct labour organisations who exceed the agreed completion date would face financial penalties under the contract.

vi) Encouraging more local authorities to **delegate management to tenant bodies.**

The job of councils is to choose the best way of providing what people want. Some councils still patronise their tenants, apparently believing that only the council itself can provide the required service. But other authorities have shown that aspects of housing management can be performed best by those outside the council's employ. **Compulsory competitive tendering will be introduced into the field of housing management** to extend this process more widely. It will be framed to accommodate tenant participation in management.

The Housing Corporation: a stronger Tenants' Guarantee

Housing associations will be the principal providers of new subsidised housing for the 1990s. The associations have extensive freedoms to run their organisations in a way which makes sense in relation to local needs. But they also take on responsibilities towards their tenants, and towards the taxpayer who funds them.

*As part of the Citizen's Charter, the Housing Corporation will issue a stronger **Tenants' Guarantee** . Like the present guarantee this will set benchmarks for assessing the quality of service on rents, allocation, maintenance and repair. But it will add three new principles of accountability:*

*● **performance information** is to*

*be produced and **made directly available to tenants;***

*● structured and regular consultation with tenants through **satisfaction surveys;***

*●more active promotion **of tenant representative organisations,** including provision of facilities and involvement in policy reviews.*

*The Tenants' Guarantee requires associations to provide their tenants with a contractual **right to carry out repairs.** It gives them the right to have the cost refunded in certain circumstances when the association has failed to carry out its obligations. We will ensure that all housing association tenants are fully aware of these rights.*

TRANSPORT

Rail in Britain: a new start

For all the efforts of staff and management, British Rail's performance too often falls short of what the public has a right to expect. We are determined to restore the status of the railways and the pride and confidence of those who work on them. But this can only be achieved if the way is opened to innovation, private investment, and competition. That is why progress towards the privatisation of the railways is integral to the Citizen's Charter.

Putting passengers first

But privatisation cannot take place immediately. In addition to further improvements in performance, passengers look to progress in three main areas from BR. They expect:

- more and clearer **information** about service targets timetables and performance;

- simple and effective **complaints** procedures;

- a straightforward system of **redress** in cases where the level of service is unacceptable.

The Citizen's Charter addresses all these issues.

- **BR will publish its passenger's charter in the autumn.** This will set out clear commitments by BR to its passengers, including targets for performance, what to do if things go wrong, and what compensation is available.

Better service to passengers

Every three years, the Secretary of State for Transport sets BR clear objectives for the quality of its service to passengers. The last set was published in 1989. For example, they include the following targets for Network SouthEast:

- *punctuality – 92 per cent of trains are to arrive within five minutes of the published time all day (88 per cent in the morning and evening peak);*

- *reliability – 99 per cent of trains should be run;*

- *cleaning – 100 per cent of trains should be cleaned inside and out every day;*

- *telephone enquiries – 95 per cent of calls should be answered within 30 seconds;*

- *waiting time at booking offices – passengers should not wait for more than three minutes (five minutes in the peak).*

- **BR will also reform its 'Conditions of Carriage',** which have been widely criticised. The guts of the current conditions are at least 40 years old. We expect the new conditions to be simple, fair and easy to understand. They will be published in November.

BR now displays daily at some stations figures for their performance on punctuality and reliability of local services. This is welcome. BR will extend this service throughout its network.

BR's performance against the service objectives directly affects the pay of BR's Chairman and Executive Board members. Pay increases for over 11,000 of BR's staff, including junior management grades, are also directly related to performance.

The restructuring of the conditions of employment of BR signal and telecommunications engineering staff has paved the way for the introduction of direct links between pay and performance for these grades, and BR is discussing with the unions further restructuring of packages for drivers, station platform staff and other key groups. The Government believes these should directly relate to recorded levels of punctuality and absenteeism wherever relevant.

BR will seek to make its service to the public friendlier and more personal. Station managers and train conductors already wear name badges, and we wish to see this practice spread to all who deal with the public.

Competitive tendering improves both quality and value for money. BR already contracts out some catering and cleaning services, and will be extending this to other activities. We will encourage BR to go further and faster with its contracting-out programme.

London Underground

Investment on a massive scale is now taking place. In the next three years alone, some £2.5 billion of capital expenditure is planned. New trains have been ordered for the Central Line and refurbished trains are being introduced on the Circle, Metropolitan, Victoria, Bakerloo and Northern Lines. The Central Line is being totally transformed. It all adds up to what is probably the biggest programme of modernisation London Underground has ever known.

London Underground has been set formal quality of service targets for achievement by April 1992. These include:

- *mileage – 98 per cent of scheduled mileage will be run;*

- *reliability – no more than 7 per cent of passengers will wait more than one and a half times the scheduled interval;*

- *cleaning – trains will be cleaned internally every day and externally every three days;*

- *ticket purchasing facilities – no more than 2 per cent of passengers will wait more than three minutes for their tickets.*

Other targets have also been set and services are being improved. Overall availability for lifts is now 94 per cent against a target of 86 per cent, compared with 75 per cent in 1988/89. For escalators, availability is 85 per cent compared with 75 per cent in 1988/89 (1 per cent below target). These targets are to be achieved by April next year.

But there is much more that can be done. Train services are still far less reliable than they should be. This leads, on the busiest lines, to acute overcrowding. Poor passenger information compounds the problem. **We will therefore be setting and publishing tough new quality of service targets and will publish London Underground's performance against them.**
These objectives will include customer satisfaction with the cleanliness of trains, the courtesy of staff and the quality of passenger information.

We will encourage London Underground to accelerate its contracting-out programme, especially cleaning and maintenance, to improve quality and value for money.

The pay for Board members of London Transport is linked to the achievement of quality of service objectives. **We will link a larger proportion of Board members' pay to the achievement of these objectives.** All London Underground managers participate in a performance bonus scheme. London Underground will be expected to increase the proportion of managers' pay which depends on performance. We want to see performance-related pay extended to drivers, guards, signalling staff and other grades whose standard of performance most directly impacts on the public. **As with BR this should relate wherever relevant to levels of punctuality and absenteeism.**

Each station displays a sign showing who is in charge and explaining how to make complaints. Information on the service targets set and standards achieved by each line will be displayed prominently and revised monthly at all stations.

The Secretary of State for Transport has statutory powers to set both BR and London Underground specific service targets. He is satisfied that these powers are adequate to enable the objectives of the Citizen's Charter to be achieved, including the development of compensation schemes.

Driving tests

Delays in obtaining driving tests used to be a chronic problem. The average waiting time was 13 weeks in 1988. It is now under eight weeks, partly through using mobile examiners where waits were longest. And the Government has set the Driving Standards Agency (DSA) the target of reducing this to six weeks by next March.

In addition, to make the arrangements more flexible, the DSA is seeking customer views on revised working methods. Depending on the results of this survey, we will expect the agency to introduce the following measures by mid-1992:

* **telephone booking;**

* **payment by credit or payment card;**

* **tests on summer evenings and Saturday afternoons;**

* **explore the feasibility of Sunday tests in some areas.**

Motorway service areas

The growing motorway system needs a full network of motorway service areas. At present the Department of Transport selects and tenders sites. The Government now intends to introduce a new system, under which private developers would select the site and build a service area, provided they obtain planning permission and a simple licence. Legislation will be needed. This further deregulation should deliver more service areas more quickly.

SETTING STANDARDS OF SERVICE

A CHARTER FOR JOBSEEKERS

The Employment Service has an extensive network of local offices. Its main purpose is to give positive help to unemployed people to assist them back to work, and pay benefits and allowances promptly and accurately to those who are entitled to them. The Citizen's Charter will reinforce the Employment Service's aim of giving unemployed people, and others who use its services such as employees and those changing jobs, the individual approach that they need:

- **details of all services** offered will be displayed in each local office;

- **national targets** for service delivery will be published each year. Performance against these targets will be published in the Employment Service's **Annual Report**;

- **local targets** for the level of service to clients will be displayed in all Jobcentres for clients to see. These will include:

- waiting times (for example for clients to see an adviser, sign on, or be given information about a job vacancy);

- how quickly the telephone will be answered;

- standards for promptness and accuracy in benefit payments;

- information relevant to the local labour market on **performance** against targets will be displayed in Jobcentres for clients to see;

- the local office network is being integrated to offer a **'one-stop shop'** in each area, bringing employment and benefit services together under one roof;

- the new integrated network will offer **pleasant, well-designed office interiors** where claimants can discuss their needs face to face with Employment Service advisers;

- **comprehensive information** on the services provided by the Employment Service is set out in a series of widely available **leaflets**, including the new **_Just the Job_**

leaflet – a comprehensive account of the wide range of services available to unemployed clients;

- some local offices offer **freephone services for jobseekers** who visit them;

- whenever possible, people coming to Jobcentres for **advisory interviews** will see the same person on each occasion;

- all full-time Jobcentres are to be open for a minimum of 36 hours a week, but local managers can decide which opening hours are most suitable for their clients, eg in some market towns **opening hours** are extended on market days;

- **annual national customer surveys** will continue to be undertaken to test views on the quality of service being provided and show where improvements are needed. They will be supplemented by **customer surveys at local level**;

- all offices will have easy to use **complaints** arrangements. The name of the local manager and of the area manager to whom they are responsible will always be displayed.

The Employment Service will publish its own charter later this year, which will set out the standards of service which unemployed people are entitled to expect.

THE CHARTER AND SOCIAL SERVICES

The Government has launched a new deal for adults' and children's social care. It gives individuals a central place in the delivery of services.

The NHS and Community Care Act introduces new community care arrangements for adults which create duties on local authorities to assess individual need. The Children Act 1989, which applies in England and Wales, has refocused services on the interests, wishes and feelings of individual children.

It requires authorities to work in partnership with parents. The Government expects local authorities to use their new powers to improve the quality of service.

For the individual needing care there will be

- **more reliable information** on available services, how to get them and how long the process can be expected to take;

- an **individual care plan** reflecting the individual's wishes as far as possible, saying what services will be available, and naming the person responsible for them;

- the assurance that **nationally promulgated quality standards** are available as a benchmark or, where suitable, are legally enforceable;

- the assurance that services will be **inspected** for quality and effectiveness **independently** of their providers;

- **independent representation** or advocacy where necessary and a new avenue for **complaints** to pursue problems, if dissatisfied.

For residential care:

- the health departments have identified and promulgated clear **standards** covering, for example, **privacy, quality of life and respect** for individuality in residential homes;

- in **children's homes**, individual rights – like access to family, personal mail and independent help or advice – are clearly prescribed by law.

THE SOCIAL SECURITY BENEFITS AGENCY

The Social Security Benefits Agency, launched in April, provides social security services including pensions, child benefit, income support, family credit, disability benefits and the social fund.

The Agency was set up to improve radically the delivery of social security benefits. It aims to treat its clients courteously, to provide information about the benefits available to them, and to handle their business promptly and efficiently. The Agency will publish a **Social Security Benefits Agency customer charter** in the autumn which will translate these principles into practice. This will mean:

• **published national targets** for the main benefit services;

• **equivalent published targets for each district.** These targets will be displayed in plain language in each office, together with the name of the person in charge. They will include standard times within which callers will be seen;

• a **published annual report**, available in each office for clients to see, which will set out how the Agency met its targets. Information on local office performance will be displayed prominently in every office;

• **clear procedures** for handling customer enquiries and difficulties, and a **customer service manager** in each office to ensure they are acted on;

• a **programme to improve service** by telephone as well as by post and in person;

• customers will normally be dealt with by **staff who can be identified by name.** Wherever it is the best way of meeting customer's requirements, a single contact point will handle each customer's business with the Agency;

• **a clean office environment**. Privacy and a reasonable level of comfort will be provided as resources allow. People do not want or expect luxurious surroundings, but visiting benefit offices should never be a daunting or demoralising experience;

• **development of more flexible opening hours**, where necessary, to meet the needs of the local community.

Information

Good information is often the key to getting the best from a service quickly. As part of the Charter programme, the Benefits Agency is investing a great deal in making sure that customers know what they are entitled to and what to do to get it. Some examples are:

• the **telephone Freeline**, which provides general information in five languages about benefits;

• specialist helplines on family credit and disability benefits: a call to the latter will enable a precompleted claim form to be

produced by computer and posted to the customer for signature;

- the new *Have Your Say* leaflet which invites customers to feed back their comments (positive or negative) on the service they have received.

Consulting customers

In early 1992 the Benefits Agency will publish the results of a national, independently conducted, customer survey covering, among other things, timeliness, courtesy of staff, and response to written and telephone enquiries. The exercise will be repeated annually so that customers' views can be taken into account and improvements can be measured and achieved.

Contributions Agency

The Social Security Contributions Agency was set up in April this year to collect employers' and employees' National Insurance contributions.

The Agency:

- holds an annual conference to consult its customers;

- will shortly publish an independent survey of its services;

- provides a Freephone advice service for employers.

It will publish two charters – a contributors' charter and an employers' charter – this summer.

Benefits and the Post Office

Social Security benefits are paid through the Post Office, banks and building societies, and the Government is anxious to ensure that customers receive a quality service at this point in the system.

An important element is customer choice: dissatisfied customers can transfer their business from one Post Office outlet, or one bank or building society, to another. The Government intends to widen this choice by extending the option of automated payment into a bank or building society account to benefits where this service is not yet available.

In addition, specific service standards are being introduced for the first time for benefit customers being served by the Post Office. The Post Office plans to publicise these standards in its branches, initially on a pilot basis in a number of outlets, and then later in all post offices. These standards will also be incorporated in the Benefits Agency customer charter.

THE POST OFFICE

Our major proposals for the Post Office include a reduction in the letter monopoly from the present level of £1 to a level much closer to the cost of a first class stamp; creation of an independent regulator and new powers for the Secretary of State to set service standards and targets and to approve redress schemes. These proposals are outlined in the section on 'delivering quality'.

Publicising local and national targets

The Post Office will in future give much greater publicity to both national and local service targets and to current performance against them. A record improvement in the reliability of first class letter deliveries nationwide was achieved last year and an even more exacting target is being set for this year.

In future, Royal Mail will provide greater local accountability by setting delivery reliability targets for its 120 postcode areas rather than its current 63 districts. And it will give greater publicity in local offices to both targets and performance achieved in each area. It will display at post offices and elsewhere guidance about the latest posting times to secure delivery within the performance specification. In addition, the Post Office will display information about the maximum time that people can reasonably be expected to wait for service at post office counters.

REVENUE DEPARTMENTS

A new **taxpayer's charter** will be published later this summer. Taxpayers should expect to be treated fairly and efficiently. The Inland Revenue and Customs and Excise work closely in partnership with taxpayers to ensure that they fully understand their rights and obligations under tax law and, in particular, what to do if they feel unfairly treated. Customs and Excise will be following up with separate specific charters for VAT and Excise Duty payers and a new traveller's charter. These will appear in the autumn.

The Inland Revenue will set and publish standards for replying to taxpayers' letters. Customs and Excise will also be expanding the use of quality of service indicators and reporting on their achievement.

Both the Inland Revenue and Customs and Excise are re-designing some of their main forms and other literature to make them easier for people to understand. A new series of leaflets will tell particular groups of people (for example small business people, pensioners and school-leavers) what kind of help and level of service each can expect from the Inland Revenue. Selected Tax Enquiry Centres will experiment with more flexible opening hours to test public demand.

The Inland Revenue will seek people's views about the service they receive. A new series of leaflets will invite comments and explain how to complain to the customer service manager if they are dissatisfied. Customs and Excise is reviewing its complaints system and will publish improved procedures this autumn.

THE POLICE

Public confidence is essential to the success of policing. The Government has encouraged community policing and the valuable extension of Neighbourhood Watch schemes. It regrets the opposition of some councils to these schemes. The 1990s will see a major initiative on quality of service. All police forces should deliver standards of service which go as far as possible to meet the expectations of the public. We want to see police forces publishing targets and indicators of performance locally.

The police service's new national statement of purpose and values sets out the general standards and quality of service the public is entitled to expect. It requires police managers to be clear about their priorities, to have measurable standards and to agree objectives with their local community. It also reinforces to all police officers the importance of a prompt, fair and courteous response to **all** members of the public.

We favour the idea of police officers being readily identifiable by name.

Response times

The public need to feel confident in the availability of the police to deal with emergencies and their speed of response.

We will expect all police forces to set and publish target times for answering telephone calls, and arriving at the scene of incidents which require rapid reaction – such as public disorder, burglaries where an intruder is present, or where there is any threat to life.

Call-out times are just one means of indicating the quality of police service. Just as important as response time is that the service should be helpful, sympathetic, and effective in all its dealings with the public. Information will be published on results of police action, as well as response times.

From this year, systematic information on quality of performance will be gathered in a number of other areas, including fair practice in cautioning and stops and searches; speed of help to victims of crime; analysis of complaints; and a range of contacts between police and their local communities. Police effectiveness will be tested in the annual round of inspection.

CRIMINAL JUSTICE AND COURTS

The Criminal Justice system provides a service to the public at large. It has many different customers: those whose interest is simply the maintenance of law and order, and those who come across the system in a particular context – witnesses, jurors, victims, probationers, the accused and prisoners. Quality of service therefore relates to a large range of situations and circumstances.

Victims of crime

Last year the Home Office published the Victims' Charter, the first public statement of the rights and expectations of victims of crime. It set standards for everyone in the criminal justice system who comes into contact with victims.

The Home Office grant to the voluntary body, Victim Support, has risen in five years from £300,000 to over £5.5million. As a result, local voluntary schemes now cover most of the population of England and Wales. They help well over half a million victims of crime referred to them by the police each year, and are developing new forms of support.

Civil action: access to the courts

A number of important jurisdictional changes are being introduced from this July to ensure that cases are dealt with at the most appropriate level. This will mean:

- *a shift of work from the High Court to the county court;*

- *a significantly greater number of cases being dealt with by a small claims arbitration procedure, much cheaper and less formal than normal court procedures;*

- *reductions in the number of times parties need to attend court;*

- *over the next two to three years, the procedures governing housing cases and administration orders (small bankruptcies) will also be improved. New systems will allow the courts to exercise tighter control over the progress of cases and reduce the opportunities for delay by one or the other party.*

Courts

Many jurors and witnesses come into contact with the courts only once. They have too often taken away a poor impression of the value placed on their time and contribution. Measures are being taken to increase awareness and receptiveness to the needs of victims, witnesses and jurors.

We are constantly seeking ways to make the courts more accessible to all who have to use them. Management of the courts will be placed under closer scrutiny. Comparative performance information is already used by managers to assess their effectiveness and suggest corrective action. The Lord Chancellor will publish details of performance standards and indicators in his Annual Report on the Court Service. Information on performance at court level will be made available to the public locally through court user committees, and more effort will be made to obtain the views of those who use the courts.

Bringing cases to court

Long delays in bringing cases to court are frequently a justified source of concern to the public. Timetables are set for bringing criminal cases to trial, and delays between committal to the Crown Court and trial are now at their lowest level for over ten years in London. But more needs to be done and further improvements will be an important objective of the Charter programme.

Efforts are being made to reduce time spent in custody on remand. The Home Secretary has announced a time limit of 56 days from first appearance to trial in the magistrates' courts, and 70 days from first appearance before magistrates to committal to the Crown Court. This change will take effect from 1 October 1991. The Government will review all the time limits for carrying forward a case, and their effectiveness in practice, over the next two years.

Jurors

For **jurors** the Citizen's Charter will greatly improve the information that they receive. In particular, we will:

- make the letter summoning them to jury service clearer and friendlier;

- make simpler and more informal the leaflet sent out with the summons to explain the functions of jurors and what they can expect to happen;

- improve the training of those responsible for receiving jurors and explaining procedures;

- review what more can be done to explain the system better to jurors, including the possibility of showing them a video when they arrive in order to explain the court process.

Jury service involves some waiting. This is because there may be challenges to the suitability of potential jurors; because of risk of illness; and because it is not always certain when a particular case will start or for how long it will last. The abolition of the right to peremptory challenge has, however, reduced the number of jurors who need to be summoned. Court staff are instructed to see that jurors are not kept waiting unnecessarily and to release as soon as possible each day those who are not required. Courts are set a **target** that jurors should sit for at least 70 per cent (85 per cent in London) of the days that they attend at court. Overall performance was 74 per cent in 1990/91. Sympathetic consideration is already given to excusing or deferring jury service to those who would be seriously inconvenienced. But, as part of the Charter programme we will review further how problems could be reduced.

One particular problem is that many defendants change their plea only when their case is about to be heard. By that stage, jurors and witnesses will have been assembled. We have therefore commissioned a study, jointly with the Law Society, the Bar and the Crown Prosecution Service, to investigate what could be done to reduce this.

As another Charter reform, the next legislative opportunity will be taken to bring forward measures which will normally allow juries considering their verdict to go home at the end of the working day. At present, a jury which has retired may not disperse, and is confined to a hotel overnight.

Witnesses

As far as witnesses in the Crown Courts are concerned, as part of the Citizen's Charter we will:

- make the **order to attend clearer** and more informal;

- ensure a **leaflet** is sent to each witness explaining what to expect when they arrive in court;

- establish an **information point** in each Crown Court centre;

- ensure, wherever possible, that witnesses in long-running cases are **called to court only when needed,** not at the outset of the case;

- review **signs** within court buildings with special attention to the possible needs of victims and witnesses;

- instruct chief clerks to **respond sympathetically** wherever possible to requests for seating from those closely linked to particular cases, particularly relatives of victims or defendants;

- allow victims who are called as witnesses to **familiarise themselves with the courtroom** surroundings before they appear in court.

The Government will encourage similar improvement in the magistrates' courts.

Prisons

All citizens are entitled to consideration, including those who offend against the law. The Mission Statement of the Prison Service undertakes to look after all prisoners with humanity and to help them lead law-abiding and useful lives.

We favour the idea of prison officers being readily identifiable by name. It is especially important in prisons that no-one is denied information to which they are entitled about decisions affecting their lives and well-being. We are therefore introducing a number of measures to ensure that prisoners receive clear and basic information from the start of their time in custody about decisions affecting them and preparations for their release.

DELIVERING QUALITY

Better quality services do not happen by accident. Improvement requires reform, innovation and tough decisions. This chapter sets out how we will build on and extend our policies of privatisation, contracting-out, local government reform, pay reform and public sector management reform to give effect to the principles of the Citizen's Charter.

PRIVATISATION AND COMPETITION

Benefits of privatisation

In 1979, the nationalised industries accounted for almost 9 per cent of GDP. Since 1979 we have privatised 46 major businesses accounting for about two-thirds of the former state sector of industry.

This has benefited the citizen as taxpayer and as consumer. It has brought:

- improvements in quality of service. Ninety-six per cent of public call boxes are now in working order, compared to 77 per cent in 1987. Gas disconnections for debt have fallen dramatically and are now lower than at any time since records were established over a decade ago;

- an increase in the range of services available to customers. Deregulation of the bus market outside London has freed the market to respond to customer requirements for bus routes, frequencies and types of service;

- industrial competitiveness. The development of a competitive electricity generating market and the competition between the regional electricity companies, generators and others to supply large users of electricity helps to ensure that the costs of UK industry remain competitive. In the first year of competition, the price of electricity to many large customers fell in real terms (ie allowing for the effects of inflation) by up to 15 per cent;

- profits instead of losses. Instead of costly subsidies for inefficient nationalised industries, the privatised companies now contribute to the Exchequer by paying taxes on profits;

- lower prices for the individual. British Gas domestic prices have fallen by 11 per cent since privatisation, and standing charges by 20 per cent. And the price control mechanism in BT's licence has meant that residential consumers have seen telephone costs fall by 12 per cent in real terms since privatisation. Further falls in real terms can be expected over the next two years.

Where competition is not practical or is slow to develop, regulation can ensure that the public interest is protected while promoting efficiency and benefits to the consumer:

- water privatisation has allowed us to separate responsibility for setting standards from responsibility for delivery. A massive investment programme is under way to raise drinking water quality standards and clean up rivers and beaches.

Transfers of work involving civil servants

When work is transferred from the Civil Service into the private sector, it is clearly right that redundancy compensation should only be paid where a genuine redundancy occurs. At the moment, in some circumstances, entitlement to redundancy compensation may technically occur even when employees continue to do the same job, and on the same terms and conditions, following transfer to the private sector.

Previously, separate legislation has normally been introduced in each privatisation to extinguish any possible claim for compensation where civil servants transfer out of the public service but do not lose their jobs. To continue in this way would seriously impede our future plans. New legislation will therefore be brought forward to solve this problem on a permanent basis.

British Rail privatisation

Privatisation is the most effective way to give customers a fair deal. **We expect to set out our detailed plans in a White Paper later this year,** based on these three principles:

- **a presumption against monopolistic structures;**

- **the ending as soon as possible of BR's monopoly in the provision of services; and**

- **the appointment of an independent regulator to ensure fair access to the railway network and fair charging for its use.**

Exposing the railways to the disciplines of the private sector will be by far the most effective way of making sure that passengers get a better deal.

Buses

During the 1980s the Government freed long-distance and local bus services (except those in London) from unnecessary regulation and sold off the National Bus Company in the form of local bus enterprises, many of them to their own managements. It also formed municipal bus operations into companies and encouraged local authorities to start selling these. In this way the Government has transformed the bus and coach industry, greatly improving its efficiency and competitiveness. Deregulation has produced an expansion of both long-distance coach and local bus services and has revolutionised the domestic travel market, making services far more responsive to the needs and wishes of the travelling public. Passengers now enjoy a far wider variety of operations and services than before.

We believe strongly that the spur of competition is the way to deliver better, more responsive services.

We now intend to extend the benefits of a deregulated bus industry to London, so that Londoners too may enjoy greater choice and variety of bus services. We shall ensure that socially necessary services continue to be provided even if they are not financially viable and that a concessionary fares scheme will continue.

We will privatise London Buses as soon as possible.

The Post Office

The Post Office is an essential part of Britain's economic and social life. Under the Citizen's Charter, we are now bringing forward major proposals for reforming the structure of postal services, to extend competition and choice for the consumer. The objective of our reforms is to improve the range, choice, reliability and value for money of postal services. We also plan to increase the power of the customer to take action when the service provided falls below a reasonable standard.

The Post Office can already lay claim to being better than other post offices in Europe for the speed and reliability of its letter services. Its charges also compare favourably with those overseas, even though it operates without subsidies. There is, however, further scope for increasing efficiency, reducing costs and improving standards of service.

We remain fully committed to the continued provision of letter services which serve every address in the United Kingdom, and which do so within an affordable, uniform tariff structure. And we recognise the importance which individuals and businesses attach to this – especially those living in rural areas.

Post Office monopoly

In 1981 we reduced the level of the postal monopoly to £1. This action led directly to the exponential growth of the private courier industry, with substantial benefits to business users in particular. Despite dire warnings at the time of the damage this would do to the Post Office, the Post Office's letter traffic has since grown by around 50 per cent. We believe that further benefits to consumers would now flow from an additional and significant liberalisation of the domestic postal market.

We therefore propose to reduce the Post Office's letter monopoly from its present level of £1 to a level much closer to that of the first class letter stamp. This will require legislation.

The key elements in our proposals are:

- **the limit on the Post Office monopoly will be lowered from £1 to a level closer to the price of a first class stamp;**

- **a new independent regulator will be established, to advise the Secretary of State for Trade and Industry on a range of issues affecting the interests of Post Office customers;**

- **performance standards will in future be set by the Secretary of State not by the Post Office;**

- **improved scope for contractors to trunk mail to final delivery offices;**

- **there will be clearer and more local information on service targets and performance against them;**

- **much better information will be provided about compensation and redress when service falls below standard;**

- **a review of the current compensation arrangements to ensure that they meet reasonable customer expectations.**

A new regulator

We also believe that the interests of customers would be furthered by creating an independent regulator with a wide remit. We shall bring forward the necessary legislative proposals to give effect to this change.

The Post Office at present publishes service standards and targets – for example on the reliability of the first class letter post – which it agrees with the Post Office Users' National Council (POUNC). Performance against those standards is independently monitored on a basis also agreed with POUNC. However, we consider that it would be more appropriate for these standards and targets to be set not by the Post Office but by the Secretary of State for Trade and Industry. He will be advised by the new regulator, who will also monitor Post Office performance against the targets. We shall introduce legislation to confer these powers on the Secretary of State.

The new regulator will also be responsible for making an independent assessment of complaints about Post Office services. He or she will advise the Secretary of State on levels of redress for service failures and on the level of access charges to the postal network in cases where there is a dispute. More generally, the regulator will have rights of access to a wide range of Post Office information. We acknowledge the valuable role that POUNC has played over the years in representing the interests of all users of the Post Office's wide range of services. We believe that it is right for POUNC to continue and to develop a close relationship with the new regulator.

Competition in the postal network

There will also be further changes to benefit customers by bringing greater competitive pressures to bear on the Post Office:

- at an early stage, there will be an extension of the existing schemes under which the Royal Mail offers discounts to large customers who wish to pre-sort their mail before handing it over to the Royal Mail for delivery. Customers will in future be able to obtain discounts not only for sorting, but also for trunking mail to the final office of delivery. To this end the Post Office will provide access to the Royal Mail local delivery network on fair terms;

- later, we expect to grant operators the same flexibility to sort and trunk mail for third parties;

- we will also consider requests to license limited specialist services to provide some competition within the Post Office monopoly, such as for the carriage of letters between particular groups of customers.

In each case, before the change is introduced, the Secretary of State for Trade and Industry will consult widely on the effects through the new regulator. He will satisfy himself that the changes would not undermine the Post Office's ability to provide a nationwide service within an affordable, uniform tariff.

In advising the Secretary of State on the progressive introduction of greater competition the regulator will be guided by the need to improve value for money in the interests of customers and taxpayers.

DELIVERING QUALITY

Roadworks

Delays caused by roadworks are always irritating, especially when lanes appear to be coned off for no apparent reason. In 1984 the Government introduced on a trial basis a technique called **'lane rental'**. This means that contractors get a bonus if they work exceptionally quickly and minimise inconvenience. They are penalised for slow work. Because of the success of this approach the Government will, under the Citizen's Charter programme, use lane rental in all suitable cases

where there is risk of significant delay to motorists. **Lane rental will be extended in 1992 to cover half of all major maintenance contracts with eventual extension to about two-thirds.**

We will ensure that in all future lane rental contracts a maximum is stipulated for the length of carriageway that can be coned off at any one time, subject to meeting safety requirements. We will also encourage the use of mobile lane closure techniques to minimise delays.

Streetworks

Each year the utilities – the gas, electricity, telecommunications and water companies – carry out millions of works which involve digging up roads. This has, for too long, been a source of annoyance and inconvenience to residents and road users alike, despite the efforts of some councils to co-ordinate activity.

So **as part of the Citizen's Charter the Government will, during 1992, bring in tough new controls under the New Roads and Street Work Act 1991.** This will ensure that streetworks are:

- properly planned and, where appropriate, combined;

- better signed and protected;

- carried out to demanding standards and without unnecessary delay.

The Act also gives the Government a reserve power to penalise work that takes longer than it should by the introduction of a charging system. We will not hesitate to use these powers if necessary.

BUYING PUBLIC SERVICES FROM THE PRIVATE SECTOR

During the 1980s, many private companies decided to concentrate on their core businesses, and to buy in services in which they had no particular expertise from specialist contractors. The advantages of this approach apply at least as much in the public sector. It helps to:

- **set standards.** Buying-in forces managers to specify measurable standards of the quality of service required, often for the first time;

- **monitor standards.** Once standards of service are specified, consumers can check that what is paid for is properly delivered and

- **ensure standards are met.** The work can be re-done if necessary at no cost to the consumer.

The objective is to secure better value and better quality. Buying-in from a contractor generally means as good or better quality services at substantially less cost. It is common for savings of 25–30 per cent to be achieved. It is generally a better way to convert taxpayers' money into consumers' services.

Where central government services have been tested in the market, 85 per cent of the work has been contracted out with overall savings on average of 25 per cent. By contrast, in local authorities and health authorities, most market-tested work has been retained to be carried out by staff directly employed by the authority.

We believe that the process of buying public services from private contractors is still only in its infancy. We propose to move the process decisively forward. There are great potential benefits to be had, both in improved quality and lower costs.

In central government, we intend to:

- remove remaining obstacles to successful contracting-out;

- subject much more work each year to market-testing than has ever been the case before.

We will publish a White Paper this autumn setting out in detail how we intend to drive forward contracting-out in both central government and the NHS.

In the NHS, competitive tendering has raised standards of performance, and released substantial funds for direct patient care. But, far too often, procedures have been excessively complex, and obstacles have been placed in the way of private sector tenderers. Tender documents and contracts should do no more than set out the description and standard of service required. As a rule, there is no need to specify **how** that standard is to be achieved. Documents which specify detailed working methods stifle innovation and enterprise, and deter potential tenderers. We intend that procedures for contracting-out in the NHS should be greatly simplified and streamlined.

We will also extend the **scope** of market-testing in the NHS. Services such as distribution, warehousing, non-emergency transport, document transfer and management services will be progressively exposed to competition.

An internal market for services

The DTI has put its central support services on a market basis. An increasing number of common services are now charged for at full economic cost, making it very easy to compare the value for money offered by the internal service with that available from outside suppliers. Managers in the department have budgets that they can choose to spend either on internal or external suppliers. This is a good model for other departments and agencies to follow.

Government research establishments

The Government's civilian research establishments are being set up as Next Steps agencies within an internal market for research and scientific and technological support services. Funds for research on behalf of the Government are in the hands of the customer departments who are free to shop around, both in the internal market and outside it, to get the best value for money.

LOCAL AUTHORITIES

Local authorities have historically seen the direct provision of services to the community as one of their major tasks. However, we believe that now is the time for a new approach. The real task for local authorities lies in setting priorities, determining the standards of service which their citizens should enjoy, and finding the best ways to meet them. By concentrating on these strategic responsibilities they will enable their communities to enjoy higher standards, more choice, better value for money and a greater degree of involvement in the decisions which affect them. The key tools by which we seek to achieve this transition are competition and accountability.

Competition

Allowing the private sector to compete to provide local authority services can bring significant improvements in value for money, either because the in-house work force improves its efficiency to match the competition, or because the private firm which wins the contract can beat the in-house staff on price and/or quality.

Some local authorities have led the way in using the private sector to deliver services to the consumer, leaving the authority free to concentrate on planning the future direction of service delivery and on setting quality standards and monitoring the service to ensure that the standard required is achieved. However, a number of other authorities have persisted in retaining all work in-house. We have therefore had to introduce compulsory competitive tendering for a significant number of services, to ensure that local taxpayers in all areas share in the benefits which competition brings.

But much remains to be done. The Government is, therefore, looking urgently at ways of extending competition further. We are examining how best to extend compulsory competitive tendering to professional local authority employees such as lawyers, accountants, architects and surveyors. We intend to ensure that private firms have a fair chance to compete for local authority work. The Government already has powers to preclude the local authority's own work force from carrying out certain activities, where it fails to meet its financial obligations or seeks to gain an unfair advantage over the private sector by other means. This could also be appropriate where an authority demonstrably fails to provide an acceptable level of service.

We are convinced that the widest possible application of competition will benefit the local taxpayer and consumer of services alike.

PERFORMANCE AND PAY

The ways in which people are paid can have a powerful effect on improving performance. Pay systems in the public sector need to make a regular and direct link between a person's contribution to the standards of service provided and his or her reward. But of course the label of 'performance pay' must not be used, as has sometimes happened in the past as a way of dressing up what would otherwise be unacceptable pay increases.

Action to achieve this objective has been taken across the public sector, including:

- new contracts for family doctors, including payments for hitting targets;

- general managers in the NHS paid according to performance, including success in tackling waiting lists;

- in schools, heads and deputies receiving more pay for improved performance;

- extra payments available for the best classroom teachers;

- in the Civil Service, performance pay related to individual performance for most staff;

- in the new agencies of government, the chief executives' pay related directly to performance and many chief executives on short term performance-linked contracts;

- nationalised industry directors eligible for bonuses which depend on the industry meeting its service targets.

But much more is required to make the links between pay, performance, and quality of service tighter and more effective. We want to see:

- more **delegation** of decisions on pay – the system of reward must be closer to the responsibility for the delivery of a service;

- **extending rewards** for performance – and, equally important, penalties for failure – as part of the normal package of pay and conditions;

- securing **value for money** for the taxpayer by tight cost control, with the net cost of performance rewards paid for by real productivity increases;

- ensuring that rewards for performance are only given when demanding **quality of service targets** have been met.

Over the coming months we want to see these principles advanced:

- we will urge the Pay Review Bodies to take performance more into account in their recommendations over successive reports, especially for those in the NHS and for teachers. This does not mean that the Review Bodies should recommend a higher increase in the pay bill than they otherwise would.

But we will expect the composition of the recommendations to change so that a larger proportion of pay would be linked to performance;

- we will encourage the drive towards greater delegation and flexibility in the Civil Service (to departments and agencies); in the NHS (through trusts); and in education (to grant-maintained schools);

- in the remaining nationalised industries we will support management's efforts to spread performance-related pay; we want to see the rewards of the top management of, for example, British Rail and the London Underground more closely linked to the delivery of improved services to the travelling public.

Driving Standards Agency bonus scheme

In the Driving Standards Agency a new bonus scheme will mean that bonus payments for driving examiners and other staff will be linked to the length of waiting times for driving tests and to the number of tests cancelled by the agency. Compensation is paid to members of the public who suffer loss when their tests are cancelled. Fewer cancellations will increase the money available for staff bonuses.

DELIVERING QUALITY

NEXT STEPS

As part of the drive towards more businesslike and decentralised delivery of services, the executive functions of central government are being handed over to Next Steps agencies. The agencies remain within government, but they are set up specifically to deliver particular services or products, such as driving licences, passports, social security benefits and so on. There is a single named individual – a chief executive – in charge who is personally responsible to ministers for delivering the service.

There are now more than 50 agencies, with more to come. The aim is that all the executive activities of government will, as far as practicable, be operating along these lines by the end of 1993. Each agency has a framework document, which states the job to be done, the lines of responsibility, and the extent of managerial independence. The document, which is published, sets out in a semi-contractual way the duties and responsibilities on both sides of the relationship between minister and chief executive. Through it, and the

corporate and annual plans which support it, ministers lay down targets for the standards of service which the agency is to deliver, and establish the chief executive's budget. Our aim is to allow as much managerial independence as possible, with reporting lines as short as possible. This is vital if we are to release the flair and innovation in the public sector that bureaucratic structures tend to stifle.

Agencies will fully comply with the principles of the Citizen's Charter:

- agency staff who deal directly with the public will normally be identified by name;

- all agencies will publish and display in public offices the standards of service which individual clients and customers can expect;

- all agencies will have published, easily understood and easy-to-use complaints procedures;

- all agencies will regularly consult customers and clients about the services they provide.

Freedom to manage

The best results will be achieved if the staff can respond directly to the needs of their clients. It is one of the main aims of Next Steps that, under the direction of ministers, chief executives should have the authority and responsibility to manage their agencies in the way best suited to their customers' needs and in order to achieve the progressive improvements in performance, quality of service and value for money that are required. The Government will introduce legislation to remove technical impediments to the delegation of decisions about how the Civil Service is managed.

A recent report by the Efficiency Unit has set out a number of ideas for developing the roles of both departments and agencies in support of ministers. Departments must provide well-informed and authoritative support in order that ministers can give agencies clear strategic direction; determine the financial resources to be made available; set robust targets for the quality of service, financial performance and efficiency; and call chief executives to account for their performance. Chief executives, on the other hand, will have increased personal responsibility and authority for running their organisations in order to achieve the progressive improvements that are required.

As agencies' track records are established, they will be given more delegations and flexibilities, provided that essential public expenditure controls are not jeopardised. As a result of this move to a more strategic role for departments, the numbers of civil servants at the centres of departments will be reduced.

NEXT STEPS SUCCESSES AGAINST TARGETS 1990/91

Driving Standards Agency

Target for 'L' test waiting times outside London, eight weeks against waits of nine weeks and eleven weeks in the previous two years. Bettered by 9 per cent. Achieved 7.3 weeks.

Land Registry

Speed and accuracy targets for handling both pre- and post-completion applications beaten. About 98 per cent of pre-completion applications handled in four days (target 90.5 per cent), helping to avoid house purchase delays. Average for post-completion applications seven weeks (target eight weeks).

Employment Service

Accuracy of unemployment benefit payments 95.2 per cent against target 95 per cent.

DVLA

Faster response rate for licence holders and telephone enquirers. 24,000 select numbers sold since Christmas start-up.

Quality management in government

Since 1982, the Government has been urging British industry to adopt a structured, systematic approach to service and product quality. This involves deciding what quality to aim for, the quality that is most cost-effective and appropriate, and then organising systems to ensure that it is delivered and maintained. Some public sector bodies and parts of government departments (for example the Information Technology Services Agency in the Department of Social Security, the Import Licensing Branch of the DTI) are using the British Standard for quality management (BS 5750) to improve the quality of their work. We expect many more to follow.

The Charter Standard will be tailored specifically to quality of service in the public sector, and will provide a further stimulus to raising standards.

DELIVERING QUALITY

CHECKING PROGRESS

AUDIT AND INSPECTION

All public services should have efficient independent arrangements for audit. As in private business, this is essential if they are to be managed well. There is a further powerful stimulus to improvement when those outside a service are able to compare the performance of one body with that of others on a clear and consistent basis. Good external audit and inspection expose weaknesses. They confirm the reliability of good internal systems. They help to spread good practice, value for money and raise the quality of service.

Auditors do not set or enforce standards. That is the job of the elected government or local authority. But rigorous and independent inspectors and auditors can perform a vital role in checking how performance compares with both local and national standards. Auditors can identify under-used or badly used assets. They have an essential role in seeing that public money is spent properly and that the resulting services are good value for money.

As part of the Charter programme, the Government proposes to strengthen audit and inspection services. Proposed legislation would require:

- local authorities to **publish their response** to auditors' reports;

- the Audit Commission to publish new **league tables of local authority performance** and similar tables for health services;

- there will be major reforms of the **Schools Inspectorate** at national and local level;

- a new independent element will be introduced into the **Inspectorate of Constabulary;**

- consultative proposals will be published later this year on strengthening the role of the **Social Services Inspectorate** and introducing an independent lay element into its work.

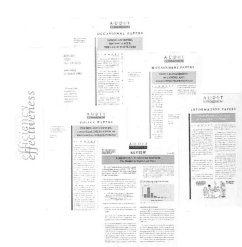

efficiency
effectiveness

Comparisons of performance

Simple comparisons of performance often show striking differences between the best and the least efficient providers of public services. The Audit Commission has observed over the years that in many areas of local government and NHS performance the difference between the top and bottom quartiles is often around three to one, and sometimes more.

*In **police work** the average number of successful identifications per finger-print officer is 93 per year. The most efficient quartile of police forces achieve over 157 while the lower quartile is only 48.*

*In **local government** the average cost of cutting a square metre of grass in county authorities is 1.9 pence. The upper and lower quartiles are 2.8 pence and 1.1 pence.*

***Community Charge** collection costs per charge-payer range from £6.25 at the lower quartile to £15.50 at the upper.*

*In **education** the average proportion of time that local schools inspectors spend in observing teaching is 18 per cent. The highest quartile is over 36 per cent and the lowest less than 6 per cent.*

*In the **NHS** the costs of commonly used sterile examination packs range from 46 pence at the lower quartile to £1.79 at the upper.*

In each case these are the ranges between the top 25 per cent and the bottom 25 per cent. The overall differences between the very best and the very worst are even more remarkable. The scope for improvement just by bringing the bottom 25 per cent up to what is currently the average is clearly very great.

Audit – how it works now

The National Audit Office audits central government and a number of organisations which receive government funding. **The Audit Commission** is the principal auditor for local government and, with the National Audit Office, for the NHS.

Both these organisations provide a financial audit. But they also do important work in improving value for money. The National Audit Office, in its value for money studies, tends to examine aspects of individual departments in depth. The Audit Commission has specialised in comparative studies which examine value for money in the services provided by a large number of local authorities.

We want to see informed, hard-hitting and imaginative audit applied as widely and openly as possible. This would help the public to understand better how good and how efficient local services are. Much of the comparative information produced by the Audit Commission has helped to do this. It has given a powerful incentive to many authorities to improve performance.

Local authority audit – a programme for reform

In the best authorities, good services are provided to a high standard. But the present disparity in standards between different local authorities means that too many people in Britain are still ill-served by their authorities, forced to accept sub-standard service. Inefficiency and waste go hand in hand with poor financial control and too little concern for the cost of services to those who pay for them.

Under the Charter programme, we want to help the auditors do an even better job in their work for the public. The Government therefore proposes to introduce legislation to remove obstacles which stop the Audit Commission exposing to the public details of how their council is doing. This would force local authorities to respond, in detail and **in public**, to the recommendations made by their auditors. The changes would enhance the role of the Audit Commission and increase the impact of its work.

Holding councils to account in public

At present, when local authorities receive a report from their auditor, they do not have to respond to it in any way. The proposed legislation would require authorities to publish a formal response to their auditor's reports. They would have to set out what action they propose to take. This response will have to be debated and approved by the full council in open session. There would be safeguards to protect genuinely confidential matters where these are raised by the auditor.

Better information

At present there is a wide gap in quality between the best local authority services and the worst. The legislation would require all authorities to publish – not only in committee agendas but in ways more accessible to the public – information which shows what standard of service they are providing at what cost. The standards would be on a common basis, to be prescribed following consultation, so the standards and costs in one authority can be easily compared with another. This information would be subject to checking by the auditor.

League tables of performance

At present there is no easy way of comparing one authority's performance with another. The Audit Commission publishes comparisons, but these do not identify individual authorities by name. Legislation will be introduced to permit the Commission to identify individual authorities. There would be safeguards to protect genuinely confidential information. Public debate about the efficiency and quality of services would as a result be much better informed. In cases of extreme inefficiency the Government would not hesitate to use its powers to close down inefficient direct labour organisations.

NHS audit

We shall also invite the Audit Commission to publish similar comparative tables for the NHS as a stimulus to improvement. These will supplement standard information for patients which health authorities are expected to provide. We would expect relatively weak health authorities to take action to bring about management improvements.

CHECKING PROGRESS

CHECKING PROGRESS

INSPECTION

The main inspectorates cover key areas of public service – police, prisons, schools, social services. The inspectorates are concerned with value for money and standards of output and performance. However, their central responsibility is to check that the professional services that the public receives are delivered in the most effective way possible and genuinely meet the needs of those whom they serve. In the past, inspectorates have often been staffed exclusively by members of the profession they oversee. Under the Citizen's Charter programme, the Government will change this balance.

The case for change
It is important that there should be a professional element to inspection. However, we believe that it is essential also that inspectors reflect the interests of the public receiving a service as well as the profession providing it. If an inspectorate is too close to the profession it is supervising there is a risk that it will lose touch with the interests of the people who use the service. It may be captured by fashionable theories and lose the independence and

objectivity that the public needs. Professional inspectorates can easily become part of a closed professional world.

The Citizen's Charter will therefore begin to open up inspectorates to the outside world. It will make them much more responsive to public concerns. To this end, we will appoint lay members to more inspectorates to work closely with professional colleagues. The lay members' job will be to ensure that the judgment of what represents good practice is not left just to the professionals – professional views will be balanced by the sound common sense of other members of the public. New insights can also be brought to inspection from the experience of those whose professional lives have taken them into other fields.

We shall encourage all the inspectorates to make a point of inviting the views of the public. We will expect them to publish signed reports which show the evidence and approach that they have used but which are free of jargon. A good report should raise public awareness and inform policy, as well as bring pressure to bear on management. Reports with a local relevance should be made widely available locally. And we will look to national inspectorates to produce comparative studies and draw together the results of local experience.

Prisons

The Prisons Inspectorate was reconstituted in 1981. It is headed by a distinguished and independent figure, who is assisted by experienced professional advisers. It has right of access to all prisons, and to the Home Secretary, to whom it reports its conclusions and recommendations. Its reports are published and available to Parliament. The Government will ensure that the Prisons Inspectorate remains strong and independent in the future.

Police

The Inspectorate of Constabulary plays a particular role in management and in setting national standards across local police forces. HM Inspectors report to the Home Secretary. But they also advise both local police authorities and chief constables on the management of forces, and on best policing practice. Each force is inspected annually; the inspector's report is given to the local police authority, and is published.

HM Inspectors are presently appointed from the ranks of chief constables. As an initial step, the Home Secretary will appoint more lay experts to the Inspectorate later this year. They will be experienced people able to support the Inspectorate in its work to improve efficiency. The Government will also encourage continuing close co-operation between the Audit Commission and the Inspectorate to identify scope for improved efficiency and quality of service.

Schools

We attach particular importance to raising standards in schools. Parents need better information to be able to exercise their rights to wider choice. This will enable more parents to exercise more pressure for higher standards in schools. In addition we want to see rigorous and independent inspection based on the widest possible range of evidence. That, too, will contribute significantly to raising quality in education.

Decisions following the review of **Her Majesty's Inspectorate of Schools** will be announced shortly. However, in line with the Citizen's Charter, the changes which result from this review will reflect these principles:

- the need for independent judgment about schools, teaching and learning based on objective inspection and analysis of performance measures;

- the need for the inspection process to involve lay members with a range of expertise and experience other than teaching or educational administration;

- the need to ensure that inspection is carried out independently of the producer interest;

- the need for those who audit professional standards to see their work as an integral part of promoting value for money.

There will be a statutory requirement for the regular inspection of schools. We envisage that a specific grant will be paid directly to schools to enable them to buy inspections with a corresponding reduction in revenue support grant to LEAs. The choice of inspectors will be left to governing bodies. There will be a requirement to distribute the results of inspections to all parents at a school plus a follow-up report a year later on the action taken. The Schools Inspectorate in Wales is also under review. We will bring forward conclusions later this summer.

Social services

The day-to-day responsibility for social services rests with local authorities who are required to set up arm's-length inspection units. But the national role of the **Social Services Inspectorate** provides an important reinforcement of those local inspection arrangements in England and an assurance that they are working properly. The Government is committed to a strong and effective Inspectorate which is fully sensitive to public concerns. We are therefore reviewing the Inspectorate's role to see how it could be further strengthened. It will introduce an independent lay element into the Inspectorate's work. Proposals on how best to achieve this will be published for consultation later this year.

COMPLAINTS AND REDRESS

COMPLAINTS

When things go wrong, there must be a swift and simple way of putting them right. People must know how to complain. They must know to whom they should complain. And they must have confidence that their complaint will be dealt with.

It is fundamental to the Citizen's Charter that all public services, including local authorities, should have clear and well-publicised complaints procedures.

Any complaints mechanism should:

• be open and accessible, and supported by clearly displayed standards at the point of service;

• provide readily available information about how to complain, and a clearly identified point of contact for doing so;

• provide a code of practice for handling complaints. This should include tight targets for resolving complaints and clear information on further procedures if the customer is not satisfied with the response.

It is usually best to resolve complaints on the spot. The more centralised and remote a complaints procedure is, the likelier it is to be slower, more expensive and less 'user friendly'. But where more than one service is provided, a central contact point – for example a telephone helpline – can be useful in giving advice about how and where to complain.

Examples of complaints procedures

NHS

• **every hospital and other unit providing health care should publicise the name, address and telephone number** *of a senior officer responsible for dealing with complaints from patients. Hospitals will have to ensure that this information is given to patients. The complaints officer will conduct a full investigation, bringing in medical advice where necessary. He or she will give the complainant a full account of the investigation, explain what went wrong and spell out what will be done about it for the future. Patients will be entitled to be told the timescale within which complaints will be resolved;*

• *if a complainant is not satisfied with the answer he or she is given, he or she can refer the matter to the Health Service Commissioner (Ombudsman). The Commissioner is empowered to investigate all complaints of a non-clinical nature and reports directly to Parliament. Hospitals will also have to give the name and telephone number of the Commissioner;*

• *the Government will consult on the possibility of an arbitration system as a simpler and quicker avenue for redress for claims of medical negligence;*

• *for the family health services, patients may choose to use informal procedures, with lay conciliators, to resolve differences and seek to restore their relationship with the practitioner. Formal procedures are also available. Patients may be represented by the Secretary of the Community Health Council if they wish.*

Prisons

• *the system for dealing with prisoners' requests and grievances has been radically reformed. Prisoners are entitled to reasoned written replies within time limits, clear lines of appeal, and a guarantee of confidential access to prison governors, their line managers, and the chairmen of boards of visitors.*

INDEPENDENT COMPLAINTS MACHINERY

Where internal complaints procedures fail, there must be an external route for taking things further. On behalf of the citizen, ombudsmen already deal with complaints of alleged injustice caused by maladministration by central government, the NHS, and local authorities. If the redress recommended is not forthcoming, the Parliamentary and Health Service Commissioners have a power to report to Parliament, in effect laying their recommendations before the highest court in the land. As a result recommendations on compensation cannot be ignored.

We have recently extended the jurisdiction of the Parliamentary Commissioner for Administration. He can now look at maladministration by the staff of the courts and tribunals administered by the Lord Chancellor's Department.

The local ombudsmen's recommendations have been ignored in 6 per cent of the cases in which maladministration has been found. When this occurs, local authorities must now explain to their electorate what happened and why, in terms approved by the ombudsman. If difficulties continue we will take the further step of introducing legislation to make the local ombudsmen's recommendations legally enforceable, as those of the Northern Ireland Complaints Commissioner already are.

Lay adjudicators

It is essential to make complaints procedures more effective by publicising them and making them easier to use. But however good the formal complaints procedures are, individuals can still sometimes be left feeling powerless and dissatisfied. The Citizen's Advice Bureaux have done good work to help people sort out their problems and tackle bureaucracy. It is frequently the small problems which cause irritation, and quite often these could be resolved very quickly if someone with time and common sense and the right authority were able to look at all the facts objectively and reach a decision.

More needs to be done to help with problems like these. **We will consult on the introduction of a new scheme under which local lay adjudicators would be appointed to deal with minor claims for redress which the body complained against has not settled in a speedy and satisfactory way.**

The adjudicators would be volunteers who are known and trusted by the local community, people with common sense and understanding of people's problems. These qualities would be more important than legal expertise or public sector experience.

They would operate in three main ways:

- they would be able to step in and make a swift common-sense decision to cut short silly and protracted arguments over redress for failure to deliver the specified level of service; or to get something done where there has been inordinate delay in solving a problem;

- they would look into cases and get action taken where complaints have been ignored, or treated off-handedly; and

- they would advise people on existing complaints procedures and help them to use these more effectively.

Individual citizens would be able to take their complaints to the adjudicators directly. There would be no need for legal representation, nor would there be complicated procedures and forms to fill in. Decisions would be reached rapidly and, because both sides would agree in advance to abide by the decisions, they would be expected to stick.

The scheme would not duplicate or replace existing complaints procedures and would not interfere with the work of the courts and other tribunals in determining legal entitlements. But public services, whose participation in the scheme would be voluntary, would be able to delegate to the adjudicators the authority to act on their behalf in relation to particular categories or complaints as determined by them.

Over the next three months we will consult widely among consumer groups, citizens' representative bodies and public service organisations. We will make a further announcement before the end of the year setting out the proposal in more detail.

Participation in such a scheme, with any costs being met from within existing resources, would be an important indicator of an organisation's commitment to the principles of the Citizen's Charter.

REGULATORS — PROTECTING THE CITIZEN

So long as there is an element of monopoly in the privatised utilities, the interests of customers must be protected. The Government's privatisation legislation therefore provides for an independent regulator for each of the utilities. Their responsibilities include fostering competition and ensuring that the utility does not exploit any monopoly position.

The regulators have powers to limit price increases, and both OFTEL and OFGAS have used these to secure real price reductions since privatisation. For example the price of BT main services, discounting inflation, is expected to fall by a further 6.25 per cent per year over the next two years as a result of a tougher price cap following action by OFTEL. OFGAS has also recently tightened the price-cap increase on British Gas from RPI - 2 per cent to RPI - 5 per cent in a year.

But the control of prices alone is not sufficient. Consumers may still face poor quality or bad service. Where competition can be introduced it will act as a powerful stimulus to improved customer care, but there are some areas, such as water, where competition is inevitably limited.

All the regulators have therefore sought to ensure that the mix of price and quality of service offered by the utilities provide value for money and match those that would be expected in a competitive market. They have generally all required or encouraged their utilities to:

- set performance standards for the utility as a whole

- provide certain guaranteed service standards for individual customers;

- compensate individual customers where those standards are not met;

- establish and publicise complaints procedures for individual customers.

These powers have secured for the customer a much better deal than was possible when the utilities were nationalised:

- BT's customers can now claim compensation if new telephone lines are not installed within two working days of the agreed date;

- guaranteed standards of service have been introduced for the electricity companies covering the keeping of appointments, the restoration of supplies after faults, providing a meter and many other services;

- there are guaranteed standards, with a swift, no-nonsense compensation scheme, in the water industry;

- OFGAS has established a comprehensive new package of key standards for British Gas's service to customers, to be introduced next April. It includes compensation for individual customers and scope to reduce tariff prices if overall achievement of the standards is inadequate.

Privatisation coupled with independent regulation has shown that utilities can respond more to customers' wishes. People now have rising expectations about the service they can expect and increasingly voice their demands. We expect the utilities to continue to improve their standards of customer service, to sharpen their procedures for handling customer complaints, and to increase public awareness of these arrangements. Progress will be monitored by the regulators and relevant consumer councils. The regulators already have considerable powers and can, if necessary, seek to incorporate many of their requirements in the licence conditions of the utility companies.

We urge the regulators to use their powers for the benefit of customers. Each regulator's formal powers on standards of service are different.

We will introduce legislation to bring the formal powers of each regulator in this area up to the levels of the strongest, including making sure that the regulators have adequate powers to require the award of compensation in response to legitimate customer complaints. This will ensure that the regulators have adequate powers:

- to set guaranteed service standards, including providing fixed appointment times for customers for whom this is important;

- to ensure that these standards can be strengthened promptly wherever needed to protect the customer;

- to require that the utility companies introduce quicker and more considerate mechanisms for dealing with customer complaints;

- to require that the utilities make customers aware of what service they can and should expect, and how to complain if they do not receive it.

COMPLAINTS AND REDRESS

IMMUNITIES

Public bodies must not be shielded from obligations to their customers and clients by special privileges and immunities. Government activities should not, for example, be immune from inspection and enforcement on such matters as health or safety regulations.

Crown immunities have been removed progressively from the NHS, and Crown bodies have increasingly been exposed to exactly the same regulatory standards as others. As a result of recent food safety and environmental legislation, if a Crown body is found to be falling below standards, enforcement authorities can go to the courts for a declaration of non-compliance, which would be followed by immediate corrective action. **The Government will follow this approach in all similar legislation in future.** Only if there are special reasons, for example connected with national security, will immunity be maintained.

The Crown has no immunity from civil liability, and can be sued for damages or breach of contract like any other body. However some bodies which do not have Crown status, such as the nationalised industries, have specific immunities which limit their liability in certain circumstances. There may also be legal conditions governing the provision of service which can make it very difficult for citizens to enforce their rights.

We will review all such limitations, and will ensure that nationalised industries do the same:

- British Rail are preparing a revision of their formal conditions of carriage to make them easier to understand and to bring out more clearly the rights their customers have;

- London Underground will review their conditions of carriage to eliminate any unreasonable curtailment of customers' rights. The views of customers will be taken into account;

- the Post Office have been asked to carry out an urgent review of their redress schemes in consultation with their Users' Council (POUNC). In future the Secretary of State for Trade and Industry will take powers to approve the Post Office's arrangements for compensation and redress.

Citizen's right to challenge unlawful industrial action

- Public services are particularly vulnerable to industrial action. Indeed, strikes in public places are often deliberately targeted on the life of the community in the hope that public opinion will put pressure on the employer to concede trade union demands. If such industrial action is unlawful the employer can seek the protection of the law to get the action halted. However, the citizen normally has no legal remedy against the organisers of an unlawful strike, even if it deprives him or her of essential services or threatens public health. **We propose to amend the law to give the citizen the right to bring legal proceedings to stop unlawful industrial action affecting the services covered by the Citizen's Charter.**

COMPLAINTS AND REDRESS

REDRESS

When public services fall well below the standard, and there is nowhere else to go, there must be some redress. It is not always compensation that the consumer wants. No-one wants money diverted from improving the service or ensuring, if possible, that a mistake is not repeated. Often, what is needed is to get the fault put right, the system corrected, or better information provided. Sometimes, a proper explanation and a genuine apology are enough. For example, patients might better accept a long wait in an out-patients clinic if they knew that the doctor had been detained on an emergency case. An apology is important both because it recognises the customer has been inconvenienced and because it acknowledges responsibility by the person concerned for inadequate performance. But in some cases, an apology will not be enough. In the most sensitive areas – hospitals, schools, railways – new systems of redress will therefore be introduced.

Waiting time guarantees

About half of all admissions to hospitals take place immediately. At present, of those patients admitted from the waiting list, half are admitted within five weeks. Of the remainder, 80 per cent are admitted within six months and 90 per cent within a year.

Nevertheless, a minority of people have to wait too long for treatment. For many others, the uncertainty as to how long they will wait is worrying as well as inconvenient.

We therefore propose that from April 1992 there should be published guaranteed maximum waiting times for in-patient or day care treatment. The initial focus will be on those treatments where waiting lists are longest, and the pain, discomfort and general reduction in quality of life are most significant. **Everywhere in the country guaranteed maximum waits will apply to the key waiting list treatments** such as hip replacement, cataracts and hernia repairs.

Guaranteed waiting times could range from over a year to only a few months. In any case, nowhere in Britain will people have to wait more than two years for any operation; should that point be reached, the guarantee arrangements will be activated whatever the treatment (with an exception for special cases such as transplants).

The DHA (or Health Board) will be responsible for ensuring that these maximum waiting times are observed. If it appears that this will not happen, the authority will contact the patient and his or her GP with specific proposals for treatment within three months. **If the original hospital cannot meet the deadline for treatment, the DHA will seek provision elsewhere** including, if appropriate, from the independent sector.

Plainly no guarantee scheme can be proof against exceptional strain such as a major disaster. Nor could it operate if the NHS were subjected to severe disruption by industrial action. **The scheme does, however, offer citizens certainty about the maximum time they will have to wait in normal circumstances, and this is an important advance.**

British Rail compensation

We have decided that better compensation arrangements for poor service are essential in the interests of the travelling public. For the season ticket holder it is the overall quality of service which is important. For the Inter-City traveller it is the individual journey that matters most. This will be the basis for compensation. **We have agreed with BR the principles of an expanded systematic compensation scheme with the following features:**

- if trains are cancelled or unreasonably delayed passengers may apply for a refund. Claims will be assessed individually;

- if passengers decide not to travel because a train has been cancelled, they will receive a full refund;

- BR will take the initiative, wherever practicable, in offering compensation to passengers rather than waiting for them to claim;

- for Inter-City passengers BR will publish details, as part of its passenger's charter, of an automatic compensation scheme for passengers with reserved seats;

- season ticket holders will receive compensation, mainly by extensions to their season tickets, for days where there is no effective service;

- we have asked BR to develop a scheme, starting with annual season ticket holders, entitling them to discounts on the renewal of season tickets to compensate them for poor service in the previous year.

London Underground

London Underground already operates a compensation scheme, but its terms are not well known. These will be publicised more widely. London Underground now aims to publish its own customer charter by 31 March next year. **It will set out the level of service the Underground aims to achieve; the minimum level of service it contracts to provide; and the compensation it will provide if it fails to deliver this service.**

Post Office

Where there is proof of loss, damage or delay in delivery, compensation (depending on the service concerned) is available at levels agreed with POUNC. The Post Office will provide much improved signposting of complaints and redress procedures, for example, in post offices and in information sent to all households in the UK. Information will also be readily available on the levels of compensation that can be expected. All Post Office personnel dealing with the public will identify themselves clearly whether in direct contact, by telephone or in correspondence. There will be improved procedures to ensure that complaints are dealt with promptly and consistently.

Ministers have asked the Post Office to draw up, in consultation with POUNC, an urgent report on the Post Office's present arrangements for redress where service fails to meet the reasonable expectations of customers. The new regulator will in due course have as one of his duties advising the Secretary of State on such arrangements

Schools

Parents already have several means of **redress** if they are not satisfied. These include:

- new approved procedures for dealing with complaints about the curriculum in all local education authorities;

- appeals on admissions of pupils to schools;

- appeals on the exclusion of pupils from schools on disciplinary grounds;

- appeals on statements of the special educational needs for pupils with disabilities;

- appeals on examinations.

Information about how to appeal about admissions must be published alongside other details of admission arrangements. Parents must also be reminded of their right to appeal when they receive a letter explaining why their child has not been offered a place at their first-choice school.

The Independent Appeals Authority for School Examinations, set up by DES in 1990, will deal with appeals that fail to be resolved within the framework of the GCSE and A/AS examining bodies' own appeals arrangements.

Under the 1988 Education Reform Act, local authorities are required to set up mechanisms for parents to make complaints about the curriculum, religious education and collective worship. Parents also have the right under the 1944 Education Act to complain to the Secretary of State that LEAs or school governing bodies are acting unreasonably or in breach of their statutory duties.

However, we are concerned that current procedures are too limited in scope and lack sufficient independent element in the hearing of complaints. **We will therefore require that a lay assessor independent of the LEA is added to appeals tribunals on admissions, exclusion, or statementing.** The assessors will have a right to report publicly to a meeting of the LEA on the overall conduct of appeals annually

COMPLAINTS AND REDRESS

RIGHT TO CHOOSE

Whenever the client can exercise a choice, the most effective form of redress is the right of exit: the decision not to accept the service provided and to go somewhere else. Wherever cost effective, public services are finding ways of introducing choice. For example:

• the NHS reforms have made it easier for patients to change doctors: the patient simply goes to a new doctor and asks to be registered;

• as a result of the recent reforms, parents who are unhappy with their child's school can express their dissatisfaction directly and powerfully by transferring their child to another school.

CONCLUSION

The Citizen's Charter White Paper follows years in which the Government has consistently sought to raise quality and widen choice in public services, and to make those services respond better to the wishes of the public. The momentum of the changes made in the 1980s will be sustained. But this White Paper now sets out a significant additional agenda for the 1990s. It imposes new obligations on public services. It gives new powers to the citizen.

The range of measures proposed in this White Paper and the introduction of a new Charter Standard will mean that consideration for the public must come first in every place where service is provided, that good service will be recognised and incompetence exposed. And radical new reforms in schools, the Post Office, hospitals, and railways will help parents and pupils, Post Office customers, patients and passengers.

The Citizen's Charter does not mean that the problems which exist in some parts of public service will be ended overnight. But it does mean they will be tackled.

The comprehensive programme set out in this White Paper will be widened and developed further. Its themes of quality, choice, standards and value for money will be fundamental to public service throughout the 1990s. The Government believes that the Citizen's Charter will bring for all those in public service new pride and satisfaction.

For the public they serve, it will bring commitment to quality, and a power to secure it, that will put Britain ahead of any country in the world.

Text pages made with recycled fibres

Printed in the United Kingdom for HMSO
Dd 0505912, 7/91, C64, 51-8238, 39462, Ord No 159526.